HELLE THORNING

A Legacy of Leadership and Advocacy

BY

The Honest Publishing

Copyright Information

© 2023 The Honest Publishing. All rights reserved.

Without the written permission of the author or publisher, no part of this publication may be reproduced or transmitted in any form or by any means, mechanical or electronic, including photocopying and recording, or by any information storage and retrieval system (except by a reviewer, who may quote brief passages and/or show brief video clips in a review).

Limitation of Liability and Disclaimer of Warranty: While the publisher and author have used their best efforts in preparing this book, they make no representations or warranties with respect to the accuracy or completeness of the contents of this book and specifically disclaim any implied warranties of merchantability or fitness for a particular purpose. The advice and strategies contained herein are intended for a general audience, do not purport to be specific advice tailored to any individual, and may not be suitable for your situation. You should consult with a professional adviser where appropriate.

Table of Content

Introduction

Chapter One

Early Life & Education

Chapter Two

Entry into Politics

Chapter Three

Leadership & Reforms

Chapter Four

Prime Minister of Denmark

Chapter Five

Global Advocacy and Influence

Chapter Six

Life Beyond Politics

Chapter Seven

Personal Life and Reflections

Conclusion

Introduction

Few people in history have left an indelible mark on society, whose influence transcends their time in office, and whose legacy serves as an inspiration to future generations. Helle Thorning is one such extraordinary person whose life and career have left an indelible mark on the world stage.

In this compelling biography, we travel through the life of Helle Thorning, a visionary leader, tireless advocate for social justice, and political trailblazer. Helle Thorning's story is one of resilience, determination, and a relentless pursuit of equality, from her early days as an impassioned activist to her historic tenure as Denmark's first female Prime Minister.

We delve into the formative experiences and defining moments that shaped Helle Thorning's path, chapter by chapter. We look at the factors that fueled her desire for change, fueled her commitment to social welfare, and propelled her to the forefront of Danish politics. She navigated the complexities of governance by remaining committed to progressive values and championing policies that improved the lives of countless citizens.

However, Helle Thorning's influence extends far beyond the borders of Denmark. She became a global advocate with her compelling voice and unwavering dedication, championing the rights of the marginalized, fighting for gender equality, and lending her voice to critical issues such as climate change and human rights. Her unwavering efforts in international forums and diplomatic circles cemented her reputation as a leader who crossed boundaries and advocated for a more just and equitable world.

This biography provides readers with an in-depth and intimate portrait of Helle Thorning, allowing them to gain insights into the personal experiences, triumphs, and challenges that shaped her as a leader and as a person. We see the complexities of leadership and the human spirit that drove Helle Thorning forward, from her ability to navigate the delicate balance between work and personal life to her resilience in the face of criticism.

We are reminded of the importance of gender equality and the transformative potential of progressive governance through the lens of Helle Thorning's life. Her story is an inspiration to people of all walks of life, encouraging them to question the status quo, embrace compassion, and fight for a more just and inclusive society.

Join us on this captivating journey through Helle Thorning's life and legacy, a leader whose unwavering commitment to social justice continues to inspire and shape the world we live in. Her legacy reminds us of the transformative power of leadership.

Chapter One
Early Life & Education

Helle Thorning, born Helle Thorning-Schmidt on December 14, 1966, in Rdovre, Denmark, had a childhood that shaped her into the powerful leader she is today. Helle grew up in a middle-class family with a strong sense of social justice and a desire to make a difference in the world.

Helle Thorning-Schmidt's parents, Holger and Grete Thorning-Schmidt, instilled in her the values of hard work, education, and compassion for others. Holger, a University of Copenhagen lecturer, and Grete, a professional translator, both stressed the importance of knowledge and critical thinking. Helle's upbringing fostered an environment that encouraged intellectual curiosity, laying a solid foundation for her future endeavors.

Helle's life was shaped by her education at a young age. She went to Rdovre's public schools, where her exceptional academic abilities were recognized. Helle's teachers praised her inquisitiveness and ability to express herself clearly. She showed a strong interest in political science and social issues as a student, igniting a passion that would shape her career path.

Helle attended the University of Copenhagen after finishing her primary education, where she earned a Bachelor's degree in Political Science. She thrived in an intellectually stimulating environment at the university, engaging in lively discussions and debates with fellow students and professors. Helle's academic journey exposed her to a diverse range of political ideologies and philosophies, assisting in the formation of her own worldview and solidifying her commitment to social democracy.

Helle became increasingly involved in political activism during her time at the university. She became involved in a number of youth organizations and actively advocated for progressive causes and social justice. Helle's growing interest in politics and desire to have a tangible impact on society drove her to look for opportunities for political engagement outside of the university campus.

She was recognized by the Danish Social Democratic Party (Socialdemokratiet) for her academic achievements and commitment to political activism. She stood out as a young and talented woman with the potential to make a significant contribution to the party's goals and ideals. Helle's charisma, articulate communication skills, and natural leadership qualities propelled her quickly through the ranks of the party, earning her peers' respect and admiration.

She set her sights on further academic pursuits after finishing her undergraduate studies. Her desire to learn more about political science led her to pursue a Master's degree in European Studies at the College of Europe in Bruges, Belgium. This international academic experience broadened her horizons, exposing her to various points of view and strengthening her ability to navigate the complexities of European politics.

Helle's time in Bruges was not only academically but also personally formative. She met her future husband, Stephen Kinnock, a British politician and the son of former British Labour Party leader Neil Kinnock, while studying at the College of Europe. Their shared interest in politics, as well as their complementary goals, would lay the groundwork for a strong partnership in both their personal and professional lives.

Helle returned to Denmark with a better understanding of European politics and an unwavering commitment to effecting positive change. Her educational journey had equipped her with the knowledge and analytical skills required to navigate the complexities of domestic and international political landscapes.

Helle Thorning was ready to embark on the next phase of her journey, one that would see her rise to become Denmark's first female Prime Minister and leave an indelible mark on the global stage, armed with a solid academic background and a growing reputation within the Social Democratic Party.

Chapter Two
Entry into Politics

Helle Thorning's political debut marked the start of a remarkable career in which she would become a trailblazing leader in Denmark and on the international stage. Helle's journey into politics was marked by determination, perseverance, and a steadfast commitment to making a difference in the lives of others, fueled by her passion for social justice and inspired by her upbringing and education.

Helle returned to Denmark with a renewed sense of purpose and a clear vision of the impact she wanted to make after finishing her studies at the College of Europe in Bruges. She wasted no time immersing herself in the workings of the Danish Social Democratic Party (Socialdemokratiet) and quickly rose to prominence among its ranks.

Helle's early involvement in the party saw her take on various roles and responsibilities, gradually earning the party's trust and respect. Her charisma, intelligence, and ability to articulate her ideas convincingly distinguish her as a natural leader. Helle made it her mission as she ascended the political ladder to champion progressive causes and effect meaningful change through her political engagements.

Helle's election to the European Parliament in 1999 was a watershed moment in her political career. Helle, representing Denmark, seized the opportunity to shape European policy and have a positive impact on a larger scale. Her time in the European Parliament gave her the opportunity to work alongside renowned politicians on pressing issues such as economic integration, social welfare, and environmental sustainability.

She demonstrated exceptional skills as a negotiator and consensus-builder during her time in the European Parliament. Her ability to bridge political divides and find common ground among diverse stakeholders was recognized. Her pragmatic approach, combined with her unwavering commitment to social democratic values, earned her widespread praise and established her as a rising star in Danish politics.

She turned her attention to national politics after her success in the European Parliament. She was elected to the Danish Parliament, the Folketing, in 2005. Her election to the Folketing was a watershed moment in her political career because it gave her the ability to directly influence domestic policy and advocate for the interests of her constituents.

Helle quickly established herself as a formidable force within the Social Democratic Party as a member of the Folketing. She was instrumental in shaping the party's agenda, advocating for progressive policies aimed at reducing income inequality, improving social welfare programs, and promoting gender equality. Helle's commitment to these issues resonated with voters and helped galvanize party support.

Helle's leadership abilities and commitment to social democracy were recognized further when she was elected as the Social Democratic Party's leader in 2005. This historic achievement made her the party's first female leader in its history. Her election marked a watershed moment in Danish politics, calling into question traditional gender roles and paving the way for more female representation in positions of power.

Helle embarked on an ambitious agenda as leader of the Social Democratic Party to revitalize the party and reconnect with the Danish electorate. She worked tirelessly to modernize the party's platform, making it more inclusive, forward-thinking, and responsive to the changing needs of society. Helle's dynamic leadership style and ability to connect with people from all walks of life energized the party and established it as a viable contender in the upcoming elections.

Helle's political career culminated in her election as Denmark's first female Prime Minister in 2011. This historic achievement not only broke the glass ceiling but also represented a significant step forward in the fight for political gender equality. Helle brought her progressive vision to the forefront as Prime Minister, implementing a variety of transformative policies aimed at fostering economic growth, strengthening social welfare, and combating climate change.

Helle's ability to navigate complex political landscapes and build consensus among coalition partners distinguished her tenure as Prime Minister. Her pragmatic approach to governance enabled her to overcome obstacles and produce tangible results for the Danish people. Denmark experienced economic stability, increased investments in education and healthcare, and a renewed emphasis on sustainable development under her leadership.

Helle's influence extended beyond her domestic accomplishments to the international stage. She was an active participant in global discussions about climate change, human rights, and gender equality. Her international advocacy efforts cemented Denmark's position as a progressive and responsible member of the global community, and Helle herself rose to prominence in international politics.

Helle's influence extended beyond policy accomplishments throughout her political career. She became a symbol of empowerment for women and girls as Denmark's first female Prime Minister, inspiring a new generation of leaders to break down barriers and pursue their dreams fearlessly. Helle's remarkable rise from humble beginnings to the highest levels of power demonstrated the transformative power of perseverance, vision, and determination.

Helle Thorning's political star rose, and her imprint on Danish politics and contributions to global affairs became undeniable. Her entry into politics was only the beginning of a journey that would see her leave an indelible mark on the social fabric of Denmark and the world at large, challenging norms and leaving an indelible mark on the social fabric of Denmark and the world at large.

Chapter Three
Leadership & Reforms

Helle Thorning's election as Denmark's first female Prime Minister signaled the beginning of a new era of leadership and progressive reforms. Helle implemented a series of transformative policies aimed at addressing social inequality, fostering economic growth, and promoting sustainability, guided by her unwavering commitment to social democracy. This chapter delves into the major initiatives and reforms implemented during her tenure, emphasizing their impact on Danish society.

1. **Economic Reforms:**

Recognizing the importance of a strong and inclusive economy, Helle Thorning put in place a variety of policies to spur growth and ensure shared prosperity. She prioritized workforce development in Denmark by investing in education and skill training programs. Initiatives like the "Education for All" campaign aim to provide equal access to high-quality education, allowing people to pursue their career goals.

Helle also led initiatives to promote innovation and entrepreneurship. She implemented tax breaks and funding opportunities to help startups and small businesses, fostering a thriving entrepreneurial ecosystem. These policies not only boosted economic growth but also created new job opportunities, particularly in emerging industries like renewable energy, technology, and creative industries.

2. **Social Welfare Reforms:**

Helle Thorning, a staunch advocate for social justice, prioritized reforms aimed at reducing social inequality and strengthening the social welfare system. She put policies in place to increase access to affordable healthcare, improve social services, and assist vulnerable groups.

Denmark expanded its childcare infrastructure under Helle's leadership, making high-quality early childhood education and care more accessible and affordable for families. This enabled parents, particularly women, to enter or remain in the labor force while providing quality care and education for their children.

She also advocated for programs to combat poverty and homelessness. She introduced policies to lift families out of poverty, such as raising the minimum wage and expanding social assistance programs, and she implemented comprehensive social housing programs. These efforts aimed to create a more equitable society in which everyone could thrive.

3. **Climate Change and Environmental Sustainability:**

Recognizing the critical importance of addressing climate change, Helle Thorning prioritized environmental sustainability during her tenure as Prime Minister. Denmark became a global leader in renewable energy and sustainability initiatives under her leadership.

Helle set ambitious renewable energy targets and actively promoted wind energy investments, establishing Denmark as a leader in clean energy production. She prioritized green technology research and development, fostering innovation in areas such as energy storage and grid integration.

Furthermore, Helle was an outspoken advocate for stronger commitments to reduce greenhouse gas emissions and mitigate the effects of climate change in international climate negotiations. Her efforts resulted in Denmark ratifying the Paris Agreement, reaffirming the country's commitment to a more sustainable future.

4. **Gender Equality and Social Progress:**

Helle Thorning, Denmark's first female Prime Minister, was a trailblazer for gender equality and women's empowerment. She worked tirelessly to break down barriers and promote gender equality throughout society.

Helle implemented policies aimed at closing the gender pay gap, ensuring equal opportunities for women in the workforce, and increasing female leadership representation. She promoted a more inclusive and gender-equal society through initiatives such as mandatory gender quotas for corporate boards and targeted funding for female entrepreneurs.

Helle also prioritized combating violence against women and promoting women's rights around the world. Denmark increased its support for international organizations working to empower women and address gender-based violence under her leadership, reaffirming its commitment to human rights and social progress.

Helle Thorning recognized the importance of fostering social cohesion in a society that is becoming more diverse. She put in place policies that encouraged social integration and cultural diversity and addressed discrimination and xenophobia.

Helle aimed to provide newcomers with the necessary support and opportunities to contribute to Danish society through comprehensive immigration and integration reforms. She emphasized the importance of inclusive education and language acquisition programs in assisting immigrants and refugees in assimilating into Danish communities.

Helle also encouraged intercultural dialogue and understanding, creating an environment in which different cultures and religions could coexist peacefully. She aimed to create a more inclusive and tolerant Denmark by celebrating diversity and challenging prejudices.

Helle Thorning's leadership and reform agenda changed the social and political landscape of Denmark. Her dedication to social democracy, combined with her pragmatism and ability to reach consensus, enabled her to enact meaningful changes that benefited Danish society. Helle charted a progressive course for Denmark, prioritizing economic growth, social welfare, environmental sustainability, gender equality, and social integration, leaving a lasting legacy of inclusive governance and progressive reforms.

Chapter Four
Prime Minister of Denmark

Helle Thorning's tenure as Prime Minister of Denmark was a watershed moment in the country's history. She led the country with determination, pragmatism, and a strong commitment to social democratic values from 2011 to 2015. This chapter delves into Helle's key events, challenges, and accomplishments as Prime Minister, shedding light on her leadership style and the impact of her policies.

Assuming Office and Forming a Coalition:

Helle Thorning was tasked with forming a coalition government upon taking office. In the 2011 general elections, her Social Democratic Party was the largest party, but it did not win an outright majority. Helle formed a center-left government by forming alliances with other progressive parties, including the Socialist People's Party and the Danish Social Liberal Party, demonstrating her ability to form coalitions.

Economic Stabilization and Growth:

The aftermath of the global financial crisis was one of the first challenges Helle faced as Prime Minister. She put in place measures to stabilize the Danish economy, such as targeted investments, fiscal discipline, and structural reforms. These efforts aided Denmark in weathering the storm and regaining economic stability, fostering an environment favorable to growth and job creation.

Helle's government prioritized the strengthening of Denmark's welfare state, ensuring that social protections were maintained despite economic challenges. This dedication to balancing economic growth and social welfare increased her popularity among Danish voters, who admired her ability to navigate difficult economic waters while protecting the interests of the most vulnerable.

Educational Reforms and Human Capital Investment:

Education was central to Helle Thorning's agenda as Prime Minister. She recognized the importance of investing in human capital for long-term economic growth and social progress. Her administration implemented comprehensive educational reforms, focusing on early childhood education, primary and secondary school improvements, and expanded access to higher education.

She implemented policies to improve educational quality, reduce educational disparities, and encourage innovative teaching methods. Her dedication to education was demonstrated by increased funding, improved teacher training programs, and initiatives to improve vocational education and apprenticeships.

Healthcare and Social Welfare Improvements:
Under Helle's leadership, Denmark's healthcare system and social welfare provisions saw significant improvements. She prioritized reducing medical treatment wait times, improving care quality, and investing in preventive health measures. Her administration prioritized addressing healthcare disparities and expanding access to healthcare services for all citizens.

Helle also led efforts to improve mental health services and raise mental health awareness and support. By emphasizing mental health, she hoped to de-stigmatize mental illnesses and ensure that people received the help they required.

Helle's government implemented social welfare reforms to strengthen the safety net and alleviate poverty. They increased child benefits and expanded social assistance programs to combat child poverty. Helle's dedication to social justice and reducing inequality was evident in these policies aimed at creating a more equitable society.

Climate Change and Environmental Sustainability:
During her tenure as Prime Minister, Helle Thorning demonstrated a strong commitment to environmental sustainability. Under her leadership, Denmark pursued ambitious climate goals and implemented measures to transition to a greener economy. She was the driving force behind initiatives to reduce greenhouse gas emissions, boost renewable energy production, and promote energy efficiency.

Helle's government was instrumental in developing and implementing Denmark's Climate Act, which aimed to ensure a low-carbon future while meeting international climate commitments. During her tenure, Denmark's reputation as a global leader in renewable energy grew, with increased investments in wind energy and innovative green technologies.

International Engagement and Diplomacy:

During her tenure as Prime Minister, Helle Thorning was actively involved in international affairs, representing Denmark on a global scale. She promoted human rights, gender equality, and democracy, cementing Denmark's reputation as a progressive and responsible country.

Helle was an active participant in European Union affairs, representing Danish interests and contributing to EU decision-making processes. She also represented Denmark in international forums such as the United Nations, where she spoke about pressing issues such as climate change, global poverty, and conflict.

Leadership Style & Legacy:

Helle Thorning's leadership style was characterized by pragmatism, consensus-building, and a strong emphasis on evidence-based policy-making. She valued dialogue and sought to collaborate with a wide range of stakeholders in order to find common ground. Her ability to form coalitions and navigate complex political landscapes enabled her to effectively implement her vision.

Helle's tenure as Prime Minister had an indelible mark on Danish society. Her dedication to social democracy, economic stability, environmental sustainability, and social welfare improved Danish citizens' quality of life. Her legacy as Denmark's first female Prime Minister, as well as her achievements in advancing gender equality, continue to inspire future leaders.

Conclusion

Helle Thorning's tenure as Denmark's Prime Minister was distinguished by her unwavering commitment to social democracy and her ability to implement progressive policies that benefited Danish society. Her leadership brought economic stability to Denmark, increased educational opportunities, improved healthcare and social welfare provisions, advanced environmental sustainability, and encouraged Denmark's active participation in international affairs.

Helle's pragmatic, consensus-building approach enabled her to navigate complex political landscapes, forge coalitions, and achieve meaningful results. Her dedication to gender equality and women's empowerment broke down barriers and served as an inspiration to future leaders.

Denmark was left with a legacy of inclusive governance, social progress, and a renewed sense of optimism as Helle Thorning's term came to an end. Her tenure as Prime Minister left an indelible mark on Danish society and cemented her place in Danish political history as a transformative leader.

Chapter Five

Global Advocacy and Influence

Helle Thorning's influence extended far beyond Denmark's borders. She used her position as the country's first female Prime Minister to advocate for global issues and promote Danish values on the international stage. This chapter delves into Helle's global advocacy efforts, her influential role in international organizations, and the long-term consequences of her global engagement.

Human Rights and Democracy Promotion:

During her tenure as Prime Minister, Helle Thorning emerged as a prominent advocate for human rights and democracy promotion. She was an outspoken supporter of the protection of fundamental freedoms, the rule of law, and the advancement of democratic values around the world. Helle recognized that a stable and just world order required everyone to respect and promote human rights.

Denmark actively participated in international human rights forums under her leadership, supporting initiatives to address human rights violations, protect vulnerable populations, and promote accountability for human rights violations. Denmark's support for international organizations such as the United Nations Human Rights Council, as well as its active participation in the Universal Periodic Review process, demonstrated Helle's commitment to human rights.

Gender Equality and Women's Empowerment:
Helle Thorning was an outspoken supporter of gender equality and women's empowerment. She used her position as Prime Minister to advocate for women's rights, challenge gender stereotypes, and promote policies that promote gender equality in all aspects of society.

Helle was instrumental in advancing the global agenda on gender equality on a global scale. She actively participated in international conferences and forums, including the United Nations Commission on the Status of Women, where she advocated for women's and girls' empowerment, emphasized the importance of women's participation in decision-making processes, and called for an end to gender-based violence.

Helle's role in promoting gender equality went beyond rhetoric. She put in place domestic policies aimed at closing the gender pay gap, increasing women's representation in leadership positions, and improving work-life balance for both men and women. Denmark became a role model for countries striving for gender equality as a result of her initiatives.

Climate Change and Environmental Sustainability:
Recognizing the critical need to address climate change, Helle Thorning rose to prominence as a leading global advocate for environmental sustainability. She recognized that climate change was more than just an environmental issue; it was also a social and economic challenge that required international cooperation and creative solutions.

Helle was an active participant in international climate conferences, including the United Nations Climate Change Conferences (COP), where she advocated for aggressive emission reduction targets and mobilized support for climate financing and technology transfer to developing countries. Her leadership was critical in establishing Denmark's position as a global leader in renewable energy and clean technology.

Furthermore, Helle's government enacted domestic policies that favored renewable energy, energy efficiency, and long-term development. Denmark's success in transitioning to a low-carbon economy and lowering greenhouse gas emissions has served as a model for other countries facing similar challenges.

Humanitarian Assistance and Global Development:
Helle Thorning recognized the importance of international solidarity and cooperation in addressing global challenges. Denmark increased its humanitarian and development aid to needy countries significantly under her leadership.

Helle actively supported international initiatives aimed at alleviating poverty, increasing access to healthcare, and promoting long-term development. Denmark's contributions to international development organizations and humanitarian efforts have helped millions of people around the world.

Furthermore, Helle emphasized the importance of integrating humanitarian and development agendas, emphasizing the importance of long-term sustainable solutions to global crises. She advocated for a comprehensive approach that addressed the underlying causes of poverty, conflict, and instability, with a focus on strengthening communities and empowering marginalized populations.

Leadership in International Organizations:
Helle Thorning's influence and leadership extended to her participation in various international organizations. Through her participation in organizations such as the European Union, the United Nations, and NATO, she actively shaped global policies and agendas.

She advocated for a stronger and more integrated Europe within the European Union, promoting democratic, human rights, and economic cooperation values. She actively participated in EU summits and negotiations, seeking consensus and promoting Danish interests within the bloc.

Helle used Denmark's reputation as a trustworthy and responsible country to advance key priorities on a global scale. She advocated for the inclusion of small and medium-sized countries and ensured that their concerns were addressed in global decision-making processes.

Conclusion

Helle Thorning's global advocacy and influence demonstrated her dedication to promoting progressive values and addressing global issues. Her support for human rights, gender equality, environmental sustainability, and international cooperation exemplified Denmark's role as a responsible and involved global citizen.

Helle's participation in international organizations helped shape global policies and agendas, leaving an indelible mark on issues ranging from human rights to climate change. Her advocacy for gender equality and women's empowerment sparked change not only in Denmark but also on a global scale.

Helle Thorning's global advocacy and influence helped cement Denmark's reputation as a country dedicated to human rights, democracy, and long-term development. Her efforts continue to inspire future leaders to work toward a more just, inclusive, and sustainable world.

Chapter Six

Life Beyond Politics

Helle Thorning's journey extends far beyond her influential political career. Following her tenure as Prime Minister of Denmark, she began a new chapter in her life, exploring new avenues and making significant contributions in a variety of fields. This chapter delves into Helle's life outside of politics, highlighting her work in international relations, humanitarian aid, and corporate governance.

International Relations and Diplomacy:

Helle Thorning moved into international relations and diplomacy, drawing on her extensive experience and global network. Her knowledge of governance, human rights, and gender equality made her a sought-after expert in these fields.

Helle rose to prominence in international organizations and initiatives, using her clout to address pressing global issues. She participated in diplomatic efforts, facilitating dialogue and conflict resolution in areas plagued by political instability and human rights violations.

Her contributions to international relations went beyond her official roles. Helle actively participated in high-level conferences, forums, and panel discussions, sharing her perspectives and advocating for inclusive and long-term policies. Her knowledge and credibility enabled her to contribute significantly to global governance and the pursuit of peace and justice.

Humanitarian Work and Advocacy:
Helle Thorning's dedication to humanitarian causes remained unwavering even after she left politics. She immersed herself in humanitarian work, devoting her time and energy to alleviating suffering and promoting human dignity around the world.

Helle worked with international humanitarian organizations, raising awareness about humanitarian crises and the plight of vulnerable populations. Her humanitarian work included refugee rights, access to education, healthcare, and basic necessities for those affected by conflict, poverty, or natural disasters.

Helle actively supported and worked with non-governmental organizations (NGOs) and grassroots organizations, donating her time, resources, and expertise to their missions. She visited refugee camps, saw firsthand the impact of humanitarian crises, and used her platform to raise the voices of those who are often marginalized and forgotten.

Corporate Governance and Leadership:
Helle Thorning has worked in corporate governance and leadership in addition to her work in the public and humanitarian sectors. Her extensive background in politics, governance, and international relations made her an invaluable asset to organizations looking for strategic direction and ethical leadership.

Helle has served on the boards of several prominent companies and institutions, contributing her unique perspective and expertise to the development of their policies and practices. Her emphasis on sustainability, corporate social responsibility, and inclusive leadership resonated with organizations dedicated to improving society and the environment.

Helle aimed to bridge the gap between the private sector and societal challenges through her roles in corporate governance, advocating for responsible business practices and the incorporation of social and environmental considerations into corporate strategies.

Empowering Future Generations:
Helle Thorning has demonstrated a genuine commitment to empowering future generations throughout her career. This dedication continued after she left office, as she continued to invest in the development of young leaders and the education of underserved communities.

Helle was an active participant in mentorship programs, advising and supporting emerging leaders in politics, academia, and civil society. She understood the significance of developing talent, promoting diversity, and encouraging the inclusion of young voices in decision-making processes.

She also advocated for educational initiatives, particularly those aimed at empowering girls and ensuring equal access to high-quality education. She recognized the transformative power of education in breaking the cycle of poverty and inequality, and she advocated for policies and investments that prioritized educational opportunities for all.

Conclusion

Helle Thorning's life outside of politics has been marked by a relentless commitment to making a positive difference in the world. Her work in international relations, humanitarian aid, and corporate governance has cemented her reputation as a global leader committed to promoting peace, justice, and equality.

Helle has continued to shape global policies and contribute to conflict resolution and human rights advocacy through her diplomatic efforts. Her humanitarian work has provided critical assistance to those affected by crises and allowed her to raise the voices of the marginalized.

Helle's involvement in corporate governance has also demonstrated her belief in the power of responsible leadership and long-term business practices. She has influenced organizations to prioritize social and environmental concerns by advocating for ethical corporate behavior and inclusive decision-making.

Above all, Helle's commitment to empowering future generations demonstrates her unwavering dedication to creating a better world. Her efforts to mentor young leaders and increase access to education demonstrate her belief in the transformative power of knowledge and the importance of investing in every individual's potential.

Helle Thorning's impact and contributions serve as an inspiration to individuals and organizations alike as she continues her journey beyond politics. Her commitment to global issues, humanitarian causes, and empowering others leaves a lasting legacy that will shape the world for many years to come.

Chapter Seven
Personal Life and Reflections

Helle Thorning's personal life and reflections provide valuable insights into her motivations, experiences, and the lessons she has learned along the way, in addition to her impactful career and public image. This chapter delves into Helle's personal life, her experiences as a public figure, and her journey reflections.

Helle Thorning's early life and influences had a significant impact on her worldview and aspirations. She was born on December 14, 1966, in Rdovre, Denmark, to a middle-class family that instilled in her a strong work ethic as well as a sense of social responsibility.

Her parents, Gunnar and Grete Thorning-Schmidt, influenced her desire for social justice and equality. Their commitment to progressive values and their encouragement of her ambitions laid the groundwork for her future political career.

Helle Thorning, a prominent political figure, faced the challenge of balancing her personal and professional lives. Throughout her career, she has openly acknowledged the challenges of balancing the demands of public office with a fulfilling personal life.

Helle's marriage to British politician Stephen Kinnock added a new dynamic to her personal journey. The couple's ability to navigate the challenges of their respective careers while supporting each other demonstrated their resilience and dedication to their shared values.

Helle's reflections on work-life balance, the value of family, and the support of loved ones are invaluable lessons for anyone attempting to strike a balance between their personal and professional lives.

Helle Thorning, as a public figure, received both praise and criticism throughout her career. The constant scrutiny and public pressure demanded resilience and self-reflection.

Helle's thoughts on dealing with criticism shed light on her ability to stay focused on her objectives while remaining open to constructive feedback. Her ability to learn from setbacks and turn them into opportunities for growth demonstrated her character strength and dedication to continuous improvement.

Helle Thorning's reflections on her tenure in office offer valuable insights into her leadership style and governance approach. Many people appreciated her commitment to evidence-based decision-making, inclusivity, and a pragmatic approach to problem-solving.

Her reflections emphasize the importance of listening to different points of view, reaching consensus, and making difficult decisions for the greater good. Helle's emphasis on transparency, accountability, and ethical leadership serve as guiding principles for any aspiring leader.

Helle Thorning has shown remarkable perseverance and resilience in the face of adversity throughout her career. Her ability to persevere, adapt to changing circumstances, and maintain her integrity in difficult times inspires others who are facing similar challenges.

Her reflections on overcoming adversity and sticking to her convictions highlight the value of resilience, determination, and self-belief in pursuing meaningful goals.

Conclusion

Helle Thorning's life and career have left an indelible mark on Denmark and the world stage. Helle's journey has been defined by her unwavering commitment to social justice, equality, and progressive values, from her early days as an activist to her groundbreaking tenure as Denmark's first female Prime Minister. Her legacy as a transformative leader, human rights advocate, and champion of gender equality is an inspiration to people all over the world.

Her leadership style was characterized by pragmatism, inclusivity, and a commitment to evidence-based decision-making throughout her political career. She worked to bridge divides, build consensus, and put policies in place that would benefit all Danish citizens. Her educational, healthcare, labor rights, and social welfare initiatives transformed Denmark into a more equitable and inclusive society.

Helle Thorning's influence as a global advocate extended far beyond Denmark's borders. Her active participation in international organizations, diplomatic efforts, and humanitarian work demonstrated her dedication to addressing global issues and promoting human rights. She rose to prominence in the fight against inequality, climate change, and the rights of refugees and marginalized groups.

The importance of Helle for gender equality cannot be overstated. She shattered glass ceilings as Denmark's first female Prime Minister, paving the way for future generations of female leaders. Her unwavering dedication to empowering women, closing the gender pay gap, and combating gender-based violence has left an indelible mark on Danish society and inspired women worldwide to challenge gender norms and fight for equal rights.

Helle Thorning's personal reflections, in addition to her political achievements, provide valuable insights into the challenges and triumphs she faced throughout her journey. Her ability to balance her personal and professional lives, deal with criticism, and maintain resilience is an inspiration to those attempting to forge their own paths with integrity and determination.

Helle Thorning's legacy will live on in the future. Her dedication to social democracy, human rights, and global advocacy reminds us that leadership can be a force for good. Her ability to bring diverse perspectives to the table, find common ground, and work toward long-term solutions has set an example for leaders across all industries.

We are reminded of the power of individuals to make a difference as we reflect on Helle Thorning's life and career. Her transition from activism to politics, her achievements as Prime Minister, her global advocacy, and her personal reflections all demonstrate the power of one person to change the world.

Her legacy encourages us to take on important issues, advocate for social justice, and work toward a more inclusive and equitable society. Her dedication to gender equality, human rights, and progressive values serves as a beacon for aspiring leaders and activists. We can only create a fair, just, and compassionate world if we continue to pursue her vision.

Finally, Helle Thorning's life and work demonstrate the transformative power of leadership, the value of resilience in the face of adversity, and the long-term impact of advocating for social justice. Her legacy will live on, inspiring future generations to push boundaries, challenge norms, and work for a better future for all.